PERCENTAGES with MOM

I0112088

MEGA SALE

WEEKEND SALE

30% 50%

SHOP NOW ▶

Written by: Tashana D. Howse & Angela Williams

Art inspired by: Morreonte Williams

Illustrated by: Aadil Khan

© 2024 Lauren Simone Publishing House

All Rights Reserved. In Accordance With The U.S. Copyright Act Of 1976, The Scanning, Uploading, And Electronic Sharing Of Any Part Of This Book Without The Permission Of The Publisher Constitutes Unlawful Piracy And Theft Of The Author's Intellectual Property. If You Would Like To Use Material From The Book (Other Than For Review Purposes), Prior Written Permission Must Be Obtained By Contacting The Publisher At laurensimonepubs@gmail.com. Thank You For Your Support Of The Author's Rights.

Library of Congress Cataloging-in-Publication Data
Tashana D. Howse & Angela Williams
Art inspired by Morreonte Williams
Illustrated by Aadil Khan
Edited by Tamira Butler-Likely

Summary:
While struggling to understand working with percentages in math class, Shanna throws in the towel. Shanna's teacher agreed that they didn't see any light at the end of the tunnel. After one experience with Shanna and her mom, something amazing happens.

ISBN-13: 978-1948071598 (Paperback)

1. Mathematics 2. Family 3. School
Title I
2024917538

www.laurensimonepubs.com
info@laurensimonepubs.com
@laurensimonepubs

THIS BOOK BELONGS TO

_____

"No, no, no!" exclaimed Shanna, a sixth grader at C. Boseman Middle School. "Working with percentages in math is just not my thing. I hate it." Shanna, who usually excels in her studies, was struggling with percentages in math class, resulting in a drop in her math grade.

Shanna's mom decided to have a chat with her teacher, Ms. Williams, to figure out how to help Shanna with her math troubles. During the meeting, the teacher explained that she had given Shanna lots of math notes and strategies to try, but nothing seemed to click.

Out of ideas, Shanna's mom reached out to Shanna's academic coach, Ms. Bella, hoping for some guidance. Coach Bella suggested a clever idea: making math percentages more relatable by connecting them to things Shanna enjoys in real life.

Shanna's mom thought for a moment, "What does Shanna love that we could tie into math percentages?"

"Ah ha! I've got it... Shopping!" Shanna and her mom both loved shopping, calling it their 'girl time.' Shanna always got excited when her mom took her shopping. Mom realized they could use math percentages to calculate discounts on items they bought.

Every time the season changed, they planned a shopping trip for new outfits. While shopping, Shanna could put her math skills from Ms. Williams's class to work. Let's go shopping!

Shanna asked, "Wait, Mom, how will we use percentages while shopping for outfits?"

"We'll be looking for discounts. At the start of each season, there are big sales on clothes. That means lots of discounts," Mom replied.

Shanna said, "Discounts, like taking away. I remember that from language arts. But how does it connect to math?"

"You'll see. Ready to give it a try?" Mom asked.

Shanna's favorite store was KIDDY'S, a go-to for kids' clothes. As they arrived at the mall, Shanna spotted signs in the store windows displaying percentages.

Shanna asked, "What do those percentage signs mean?"

Mom replied, "Those signs show discounts. Items with those tags are on sale."

"Oh! So 10% off means 10% less than the original price?"

"Exactly! We'll use your percentage skills to figure out the discounted prices."

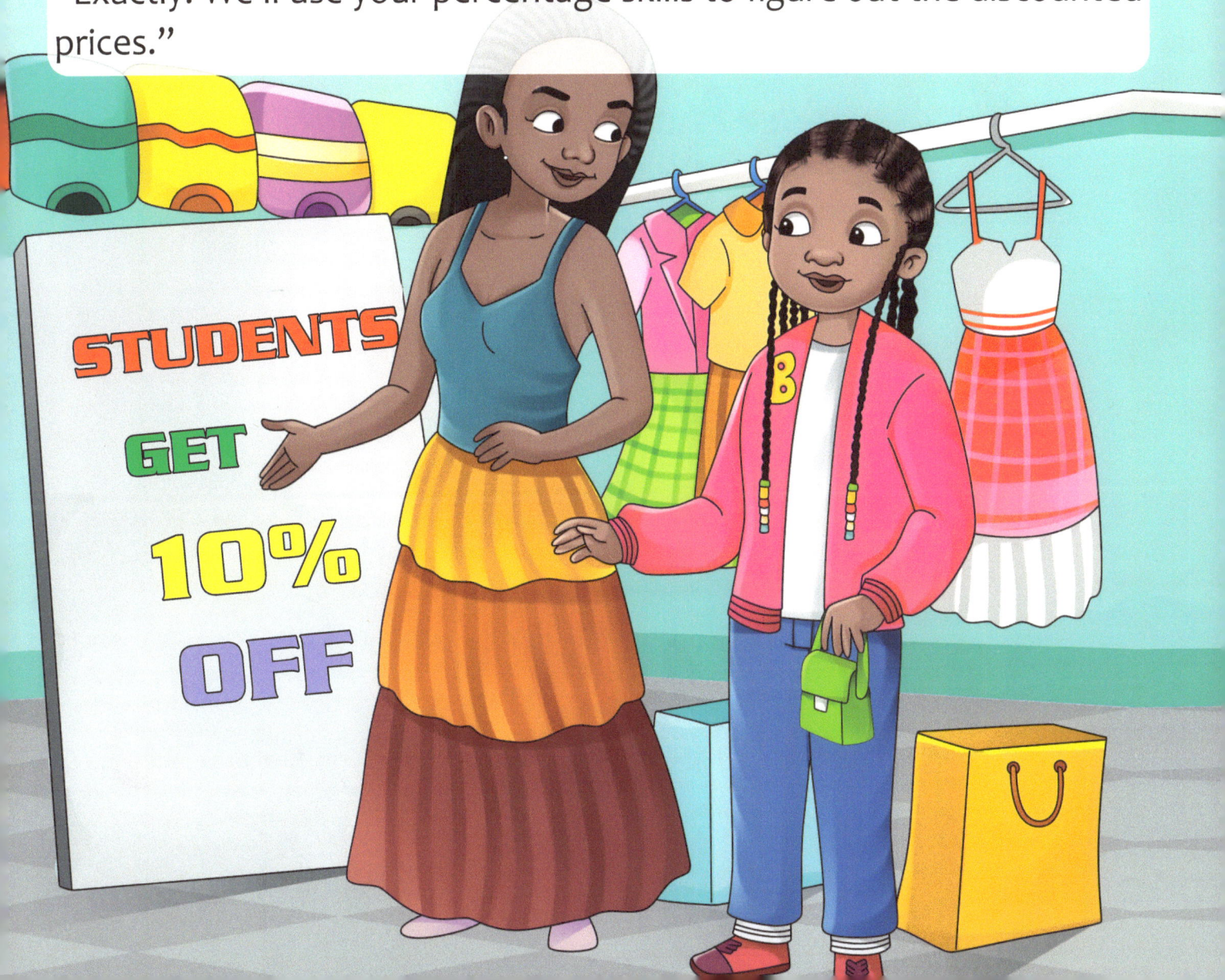

STUDENTS
GET
10%
OFF

Shanna remembered what she learned in class about finding percentages of numbers and was eager to apply it.

Shanna thought to herself,
In class, I learned that
10% of 8 is .10 x 8 = .8
10% of 16 is .10 x 16 = 1.6
10% of 24 is .10 x 24 = 2.4
10% of 104 is .10 x 104 = 10.4
10% of 1008 is .10 x 1008 = 100.8

Following this pattern, the decimal moves left by one place to give 10%.

"Great job, Shanna! Let's see if you can calculate the discounted price of this shirt."

"Look, Mom, this hat matches the shirt you're holding!"

"I see! Here are the regular prices for both. Can you work out the discounted prices?"

Hat: $12.00 on sale with 10% discount

Shirt: $16.00 on sale with 20% discount

Shanna's calculations for the hat and shirt:

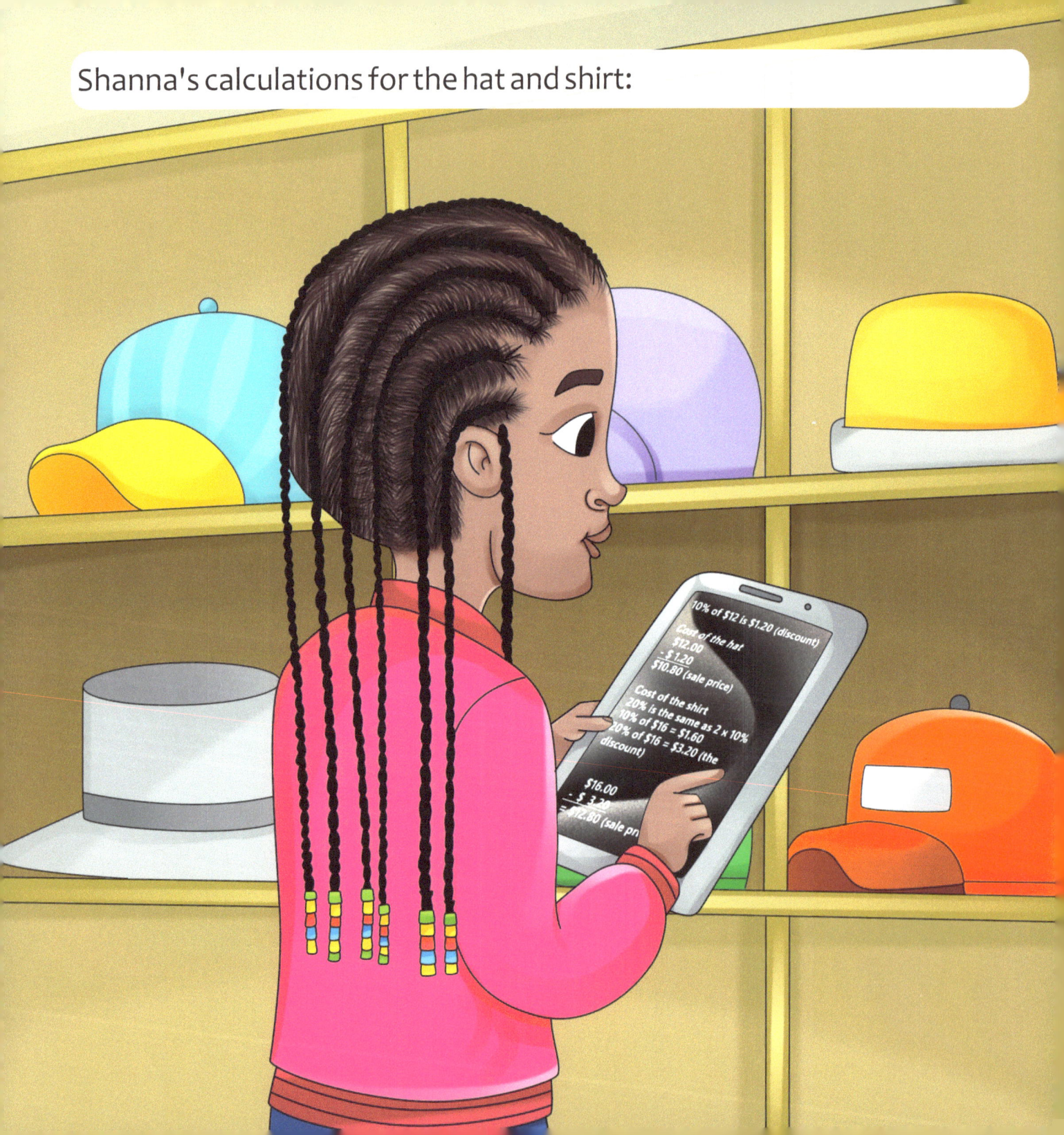

10% of $12 is $1.20 (discount)

Cost of the hat
$12.00
- $1.20
$10.80 (sale price)

Cost of the shirt
20% is the same as 2 × 10%
10% of $16 = $1.60
20% of $16 = $3.20 (the discount)

$16.00
- $3.20
= $12.80 (sale price)

"Well done, Shanna! Place those items in the cart. Let's keep shopping for some shoes."

As they continued shopping, Shanna found a pair of sneakers she loved.

Mom asked the salesman to bring a pair of the sneakers in Shanna's size. The salesman mentioned they were $48.00 with a 50% discount. Shanna eagerly calculated the sale price.

Shanna's calculation of the cost of the sneakers:

50% is the same as 5 × 10%

Since 10% of $48 = $4.80

Then the amount of the discount is 5 × 4.80 = $24.00

Mom said, "Shanna, you're doing fantastic! Here is another way to think about 50%. I relate it to half, so half of 100. Therefore, 50% of $48 is $24.00.

"That's a cool and quick way to think about it, mom. I want to try it and share the strategy with my classmates," Shanna replied.

"Your teacher would love that, Shanna," Mom shared. "Place those sneakers in the cart. Would you like anything else?"

Shanna replied, "Thanks, Mom! Can I get some sunglasses too?"

Mom agreed and Shanna tried on sunglasses.

Will you help Shanna calculate which glasses are the best price?

Blue sunglasses: $35.00 on sale for 30% off

Red Sunglasses: $54.00 on sale for 50% off

Shanna's quick math skills helped her figure out the better deal.

Blue sunglasses: 30% is the same as 3 x 10%

10% of $35 = $3.50

So, 3 x $3.50 = $10.50 (Discount)

Therefore, the cost of blue sunglasses is: $35 - $10.50 = $24.50

Calculations for Red Sunglasses

50% is the same as 5 x 10%

10% of $54 = $5.40

5 x $5.40 = $27.00

Therefore, the cost of red sunglasses is: $54 - $27.00.

To herself, Shanna says, "Since this discount is the same as the sneakers, 50%, I can try to calculate it Mom's way too. Fifty percent is half of 100%, so half of $54 is $27. Wow, I got the same thing!"

So the blue glasses have the better price!

JOGGERS

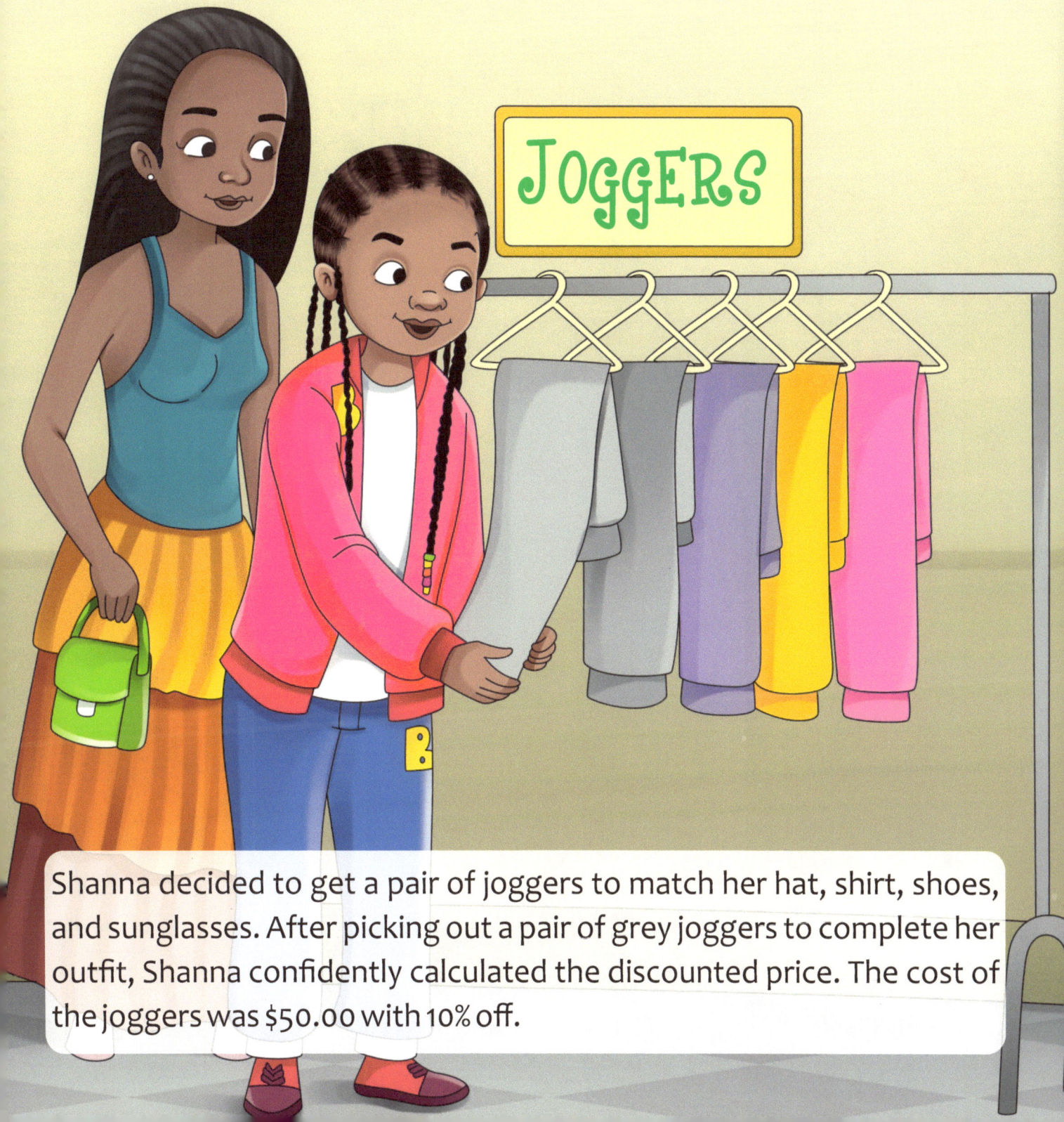

Shanna decided to get a pair of joggers to match her hat, shirt, shoes, and sunglasses. After picking out a pair of grey joggers to complete her outfit, Shanna confidently calculated the discounted price. The cost of the joggers was $50.00 with 10% off.

"Okay, Mom! First we need to find 10% of $50.00, which is $5.00. So, the joggers will be $45.00, right?"

Mom beamed with pride at Shanna's grasp of percentages.

Since they were done shopping, Shanna added the price of each item in the cart to find the total cost. The receipt should look like this!

Hat	
Shirt	10.80
Sneakers	12.80
Glasses	24
Joggers	24.50
	45

Shanna's mom paid a total of $117.10 for all the items from KIDDY'S. Shanna was happy with her new outfit. Before leaving the mall, Shanna put on her hat and sunglasses.

"Girl time is fun," Shanna stated.

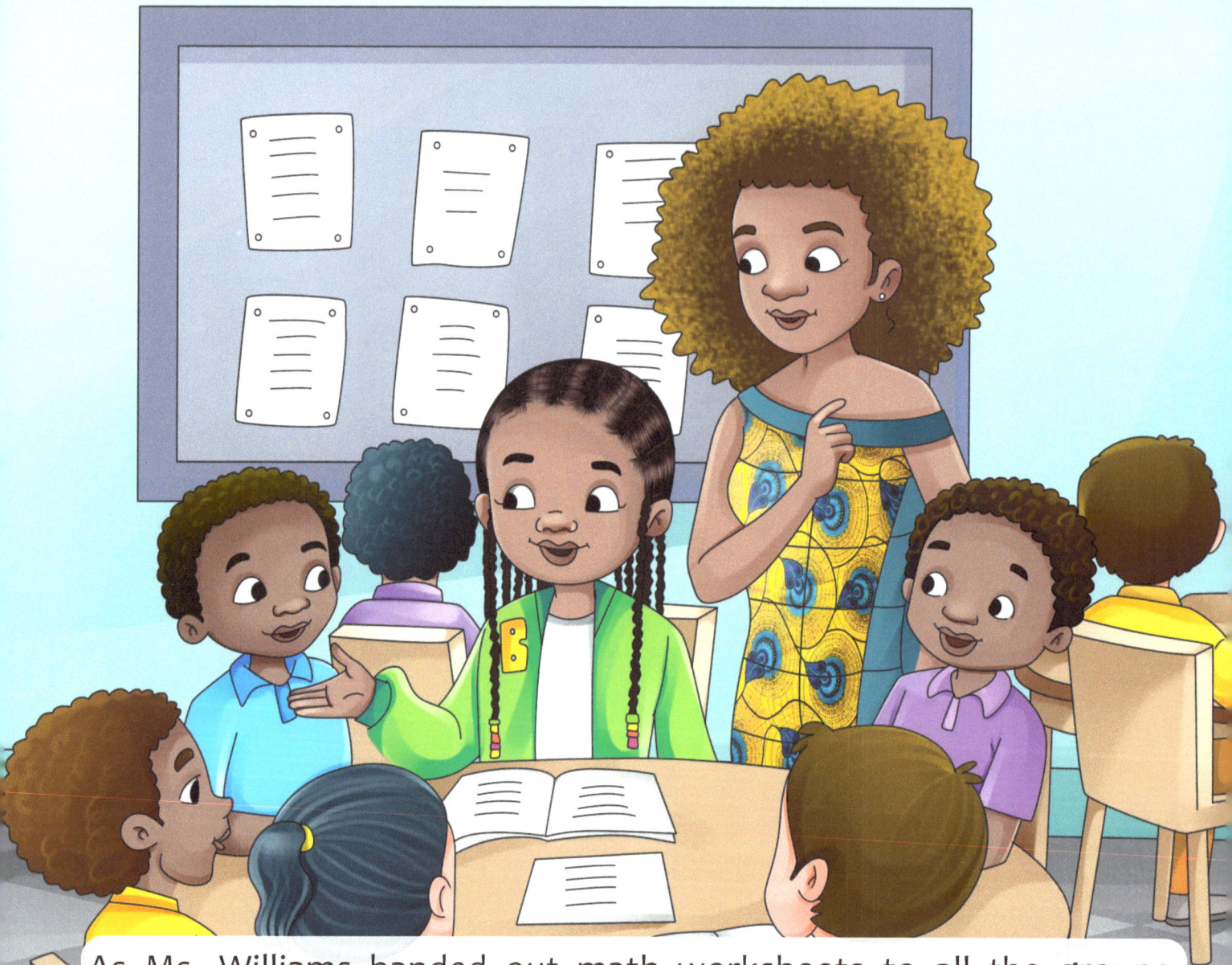

As Ms. Williams handed out math worksheets to all the groups, students eagerly dove into their work. Moving around the classroom, Ms. Williams noticed Shanna patiently guiding her classmates through the steps to tackle the problems. Impressed by Shanna's helpfulness, Ms. Williams invited her to stay behind after class.

After the bell rang, Ms. Williams approached Shanna and asked her to share her secret for understanding percentages. Shanna recounted her shopping adventure with her mom, where she applied percentages to something she loved—shopping. Shanna's experience showed Ms. Williams the importance of making learning relevant to students' lives, reminding her that understanding percentages can be as easy as a day of shopping.

READING COMPREHENSION

1. What did Shanna struggle with?

   _____

2. Name three things Shanna's mom did to help her.

   _____

3. What is a percentage?

   _____

4. What is a discount?

   _____

5. What are other ways you can use percentages in your daily life?

   _____

Answers
1. Percentages
2. Conference with teacher and coach and went shopping
3. A number expressed as a fraction of 100
4. The deduction from the original cost of an item
5. Calculating tips for service, sales tax on items, or interest at the bank

MATH

Practice what you learned!

Activity 1: Calculate the amount Shanna and her mom saved at KIDDY'S

Item	Amount of Discount
Hat	
Shirt	
Sneakers	
Blue Sunglasses	
Red Sunglasses	
Joggers	
Total Saved	

Activity 2: Solve each problem below

Problem	Answer
60% of $32	
40% of $90	
15% of $24	
50% of $150	
25% of $68	
75% of $240	

Answers
1. Savings: $70.90
2. 19.20; 36; 3.60; 75; 17; 180

ABOUT THE AUTHORS

Dr. Tashana D. Howse is the Director of Educational Services for the Stellar Diverse Student Achievement Center and CEO of TDH Educational Enterprises. She is also a professor of mathematics education at Georgia Gwinnett College. Tashana's background comprises over 20 years of leadership and teaching in education. She has a passion for providing youth with experiences that maximize their potential as a learner and as a citizen. To improve efforts in advancing the field of mathematics education, Dr. Howse conducts professional development for mathematics teachers throughout the United States. Tashana received both a bachelor's and master's of science degree in mathematics education from Florida State University. She completed her doctor of philosophy degree in mathematics education from the University of Central Florida.

With over 15 years in education, there is one thing that will never remain constant, Change! After graduating from Florida State University, Angela began her teaching career in Palm Beach County at Carver Middle School. At Carver, she taught reading to level 1 students. During her second year of teaching, she began working for Broward County School at Pompano Beach Middle School. As an English teacher to eighth grade students, Angela gained a hunger for deepening her knowledge in curriculum and instructional practices. So, she received her master's degree in curriculum and instruction two years later. Once she obtained her master's degree, she became a Department Chair for Language Arts and Reading. While leading both departments, Angela gained a hunger for delivering professional development. In addition to training for Broward County Schools, she also trains with Solution Tree and Unbound Ed across various states.

ABOUT THE ARTISTS

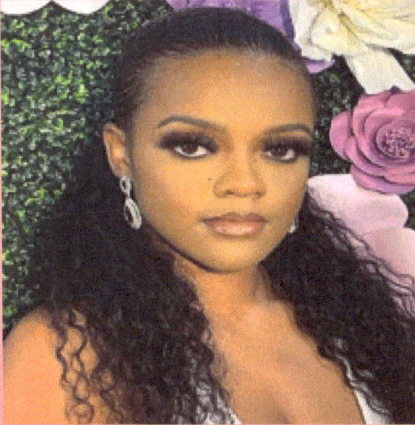

Morreonte Williams is from Deerfield Beach, Florida, where she was born and raised. She graduated from Deerfield Beach High School with a passion for art and design. With this passion, she created a business that focuses on photography and graphic design. She designed the storyboard for *Percentages with Mom.*

Aadil Khan was born in Meerut, India, and lives in Delhi, India. He is an experienced graphic designer with a love for illustrating children's books. He owns his own company (Kidillus), where he uses the latest trends in illustration. He provides a complete service from designing covers and illustrations to layout design and typesetting. When he is not working, he is spending time with family, traveling, or enjoying sports, specifically racing.

CONNECT WITH US

SCAN HERE

CONTACT & CONNECT

www.ingramcontent.com/pod-product-compliance
Lightning Source LLC
LaVergne TN
LVHW072132070426
835513LV00002B/72